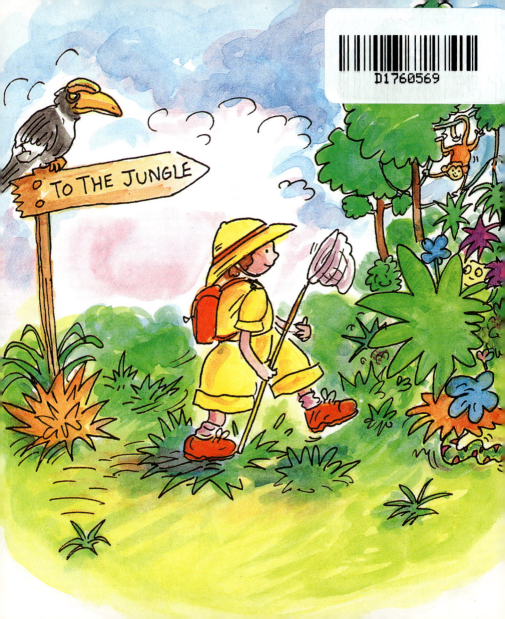

TO THE JUNGLE

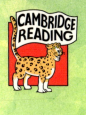

Walking in the Jungle

Richard Brown and Kate Ruttle
Illustrated by Stella Voce

Cambridge Reading

General Editors

Richard Brown and Kate Ruttle

Consultant Editor

Jean Glasberg

Published by the Press Syndicate of the University of Cambridge
The Pitt Building, Trumpington Street, Cambridge CB2 1RP
40 West 20th Street, New York, NY 10011-4211, USA
10 Stamford Road, Oakleigh, Melbourne 3166, Australia

Walking in the Jungle
This adaptation of *Walking in the Jungle* © Richard Brown and Kate Ruttle
1996
Illustrations © Stella Voce 1996

Printed in Great Britain at the University Press, Cambridge

A catalogue record for this book is available from the British Library

ISBN 0 521 46848 5 paperback

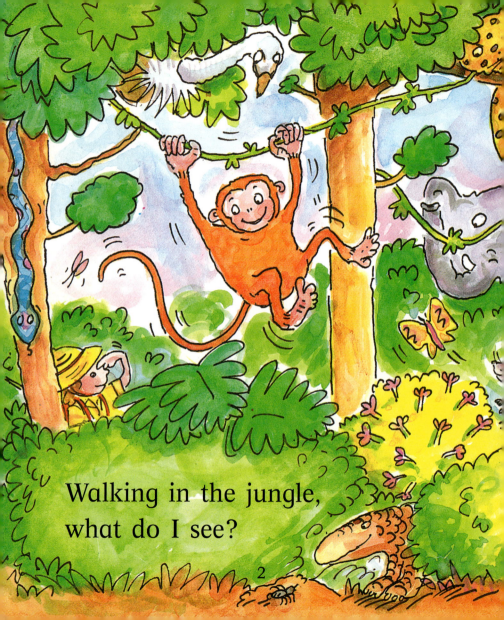

Walking in the jungle,
what do I see?

2

A long snake looking at
me, me, me.

Walking in the jungle,
what do I see?

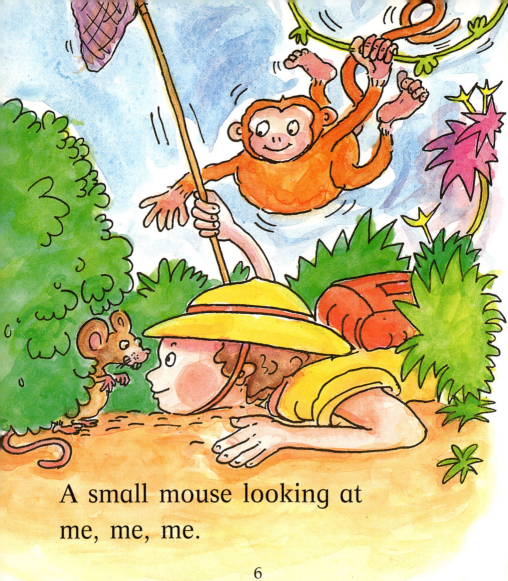

A small mouse looking at
me, me, me.

Walking in the jungle,
what do I see?

A big tiger looking for her
tea, tea, tea!